DOGS SET IV

Basset Hounds

Cari Meister
ABDO Publishing Company

visit us at
www.abdopub.com

Published by ABDO Publishing Company, 4940 Viking Drive, Suite 622, Edina, Minnesota 55435. Copyright © 2001 Abdo Consulting Group, Inc. International copyrights reserved in all countries. No part of this book may be reproduced in any form without written permission from the publisher.

Printed in the United States.

Cover Photo: Ron Kimball Studios
Interior Photos: Corbis (pages 5, 9, 13, 17), Ron Kimball Studios (pages 7, 11, 15, 19, 21)

Editors: Bob Italia, Tamara L. Britton, Kate A. Furlong, Christine Fournier
Art Direction: Neil Klinepier

Library of Congress Cataloging-in-Publication Data

Meister, Cari.
    Basset hounds / Cari Meister.
       p. cm. -- (Dogs. Set IV)
    Includes bibliographical references (p.).
    ISBN 1-57765-478-1
      1. Basset hound--Juvenile literature. [1. Basset hound. 2. Dogs. 3. Pets.] I. Title

    SF429.B2 M45 2001
    636.753'6--dc21

                                                                        00-045382

Contents

The Dog Family

Dogs and wolves belong to the same **family**, called Canidae. Other animals in this family include foxes, jackals, and wild dogs. These animals share many of the same **traits**.

Dogs have been living with humans for the last 10,000 years. Today, millions of dogs live in the world. There are over 400 different dog breeds.

One of these breeds is the basset hound. The basset is a scent hound. This means it has an excellent sense of smell. The basset was bred to hunt small animals using its powerful sense of smell.

The basset's expressive face makes it a popular breed.

Basset Hounds

The basset hound has been around since the 1500s. It was first bred in France. It was bred to trail small animals, such as rabbits.

Bassets were bred with short legs. This allowed a basset to keep its nose close to the ground without getting tired. A basset's short legs also made it slow. This allowed hunters to easily keep up with bassets.

By the late 1800s, basset hounds had made their way to England and the U.S. At first, they were mostly used in packs for hunting. Today, basset hounds are popular pets and show dogs, too.

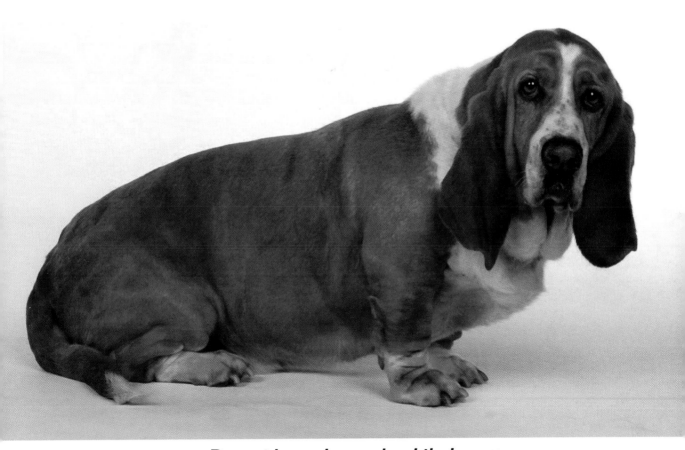

Basset hounds received their name because they were so low to the ground. In French, the word bas *means "low."*

What They're Like

Basset hounds are friendly dogs that love children. They love affection and need constant attention. If left alone too long, bassets sometimes howl.

Bassets are clownish dogs. They make their owners laugh a lot. With their long ears and droopy eyes, they make silly faces to go along with their silly behavior.

Bassets are smart dogs. But they can be very stubborn. This makes it hard for them to be trained. So basset owners must be patient during training sessions.

Bassets like to do things in their own time and in their own way.

Coat and Color

The basset hound has a hard, smooth coat. It has short, dense hair. A basset's coat is useful when hunting. It protects the basset from the scrapes of branches and weeds in the field.

Underneath their coats, basset hounds have loose skin. The loose wrinkles around a basset's nose help gather scents.

Basset hounds come in many different shades of black, brown, and white. Some bassets are a light brown color called lemon. Some are a reddish color.

Always check your basset's coat for ticks, thorns, or scratches after it has been outside.

Size

Bassets may look like small dogs. But they are not. Bassets are really large dogs with short legs. Most bassets stand about 14 inches (36 cm) tall at the shoulder. But they can weigh more than 50 pounds (23 kg).

Bassets have a large head and **muzzle**. They have large, droopy eyes that are usually brown. Most basset hounds have a black nose. A basset's dark lips hang in loose **flews**. This means lots of drool!

Bassets have very long ears. When bassets are trailing, their ears often drag on the ground and stir up scents. The large folds of skin on their jaws hold the scents close to their noses.

The basset's build makes it a great dog for trailing small animals. Only the bloodhound has a more powerful sense of smell.

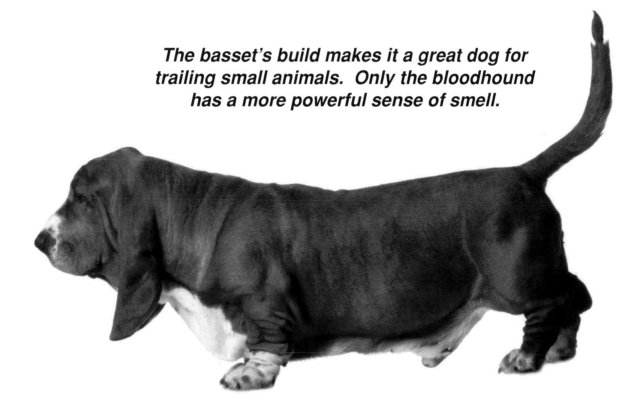

Care

Basset hounds make great companion dogs. They love to be around people. They are happiest when near those they love.

Besides love, a basset needs food, water, exercise, shots, and a warm place to sleep. Compared to other dogs, basset hounds do not need much exercise. A few short walks every day are enough to keep a basset fit.

Basset hounds have long ears. They can become **infected** easily. It is important to keep a basset's ears clean. A **veterinarian** can show you the best way to do this.

Bassets have short hair. But they still need to be **groomed**. Make sure a basset's coat is clean and dry. Bassets do not need to be bathed very often.

A basset's ears require special care.

Feeding

Bassets need to be fed around the same time every day. They will get used to eating at that time. If a basset is fed at a different time, its stomach can become upset.

Bassets need a meaty dog food. Puppies should be fed the same kind of dog food the breeder gave them. This makes it easier on the puppy's stomach.

Do not overfeed bassets. Because they do not need much exercise, they often become fat. Being overweight is bad for a basset's spine and legs.

Bassets, like all dogs, drink lots of water. A basset should always have a fresh bowl of water next to its food dish.

*It is important to keep your
basset's food dish clean.*

Things They Need

Bassets have strong jaws. They should have some strong chewing toys and bones. This will prevent your basset from chewing shoes, pillows, and furniture.

Every basset needs a quiet place to rest. A dog bed or blanket in a corner of a room makes a nice spot.

It is best to keep bassets in a fenced yard. Once a basset is trailing a scent, there is no stopping it! Bassets can wander miles from home because they are following a scent.

Like all dogs, bassets need a dog tag. The dog tag tells the dog's name and the owner's phone number. That way, if a basset is lost, its owner can be found.

A basset on the go!

Puppies

A basset hound that is going to have puppies will sleep a lot. It is important that there is a quiet, dark spot for her to rest.

When basset hounds are born, they are blind, deaf, and small. They depend on their mother for everything. Their mother's milk gives them all of the **nutrients** they need. She licks them to clean them. She nuzzles them to keep them warm.

Puppies grow fast. In about ten days, their eyes will open. A few days later, they will begin to hear. When a basset is five to six weeks old, it will be **weaned**.

Opposite page: Basset hound puppies need lots of exercise, but they also need lots of rest.

Glossary

family: a group that scientists use to classify similar plants and animals. It ranks above a genus and below an order.

flews: the long, hanging lips of a dog.

groom: to clean and condition.

infect: to cause a sickness due to contact with germs.

muzzle: the jaws and nose of an animal; snout.

nutrients: important parts of a diet that all living things need to survive.

trait: a feature of an animal.

veterinarian: a person with medical training who cares for animals.

wean: to accustom to taking food other than mother's milk.

Internet Sites

American Kennel Club
http://www.akc.org
This Web site from the American Kennel Club presents information on basset hounds and other purebred dogs. Visit the kids' corner, learn about upcoming shows, and read about buying a puppy.

The Basset Hound Club of America
http://www.basset-bhca.org/
The Basset Hound Club of America's Web site presents a history of the basset hound in the U.S. It also has information about dog shows and basset hound adoptions.

These sites are subject to change. Go to your favorite search engine and type in basset hound for more sites.

Index